AF480915

Brenda Novak

no again ?

Illustrated by Pablo Ortega López

NEW YORK TIMES BESTSELLING AUTHOR
Brenda Novak
no again?
Illustrated by Pablo Ortega López

I wanted to climb the tree in my front yard...
... and perch on the
very top like a bird...
... or a bat.

6

I wanted to be a huge dinosaur,
roaring at the top of my lungs
while tearing through the pantry
gobbling up cookies.

But my mother said, "No.
You have to eat your peas.
N-O means *no*."

11

My little sister and I wanted to be knights, standing back to back, while using our swords to protect our king.

But our babysitter marched into the room and said, "Where did you get those tree branches? N-O means *no*."

I wanted to be a powerful
wizard with a magic wand...

16

... who leads his people
on a grand adventure.

But my teacher said, "Excuse me. You need to pay attention in class. N-O means *no*."

"I don't like that word, I told my mother. I never want to hear it again."

22

23

"No is *not* a good word," I told her.

"No means I never get to
do anything I want."

"No is what kept you from fall-
ing from the tree and breaking
an arm or a leg."

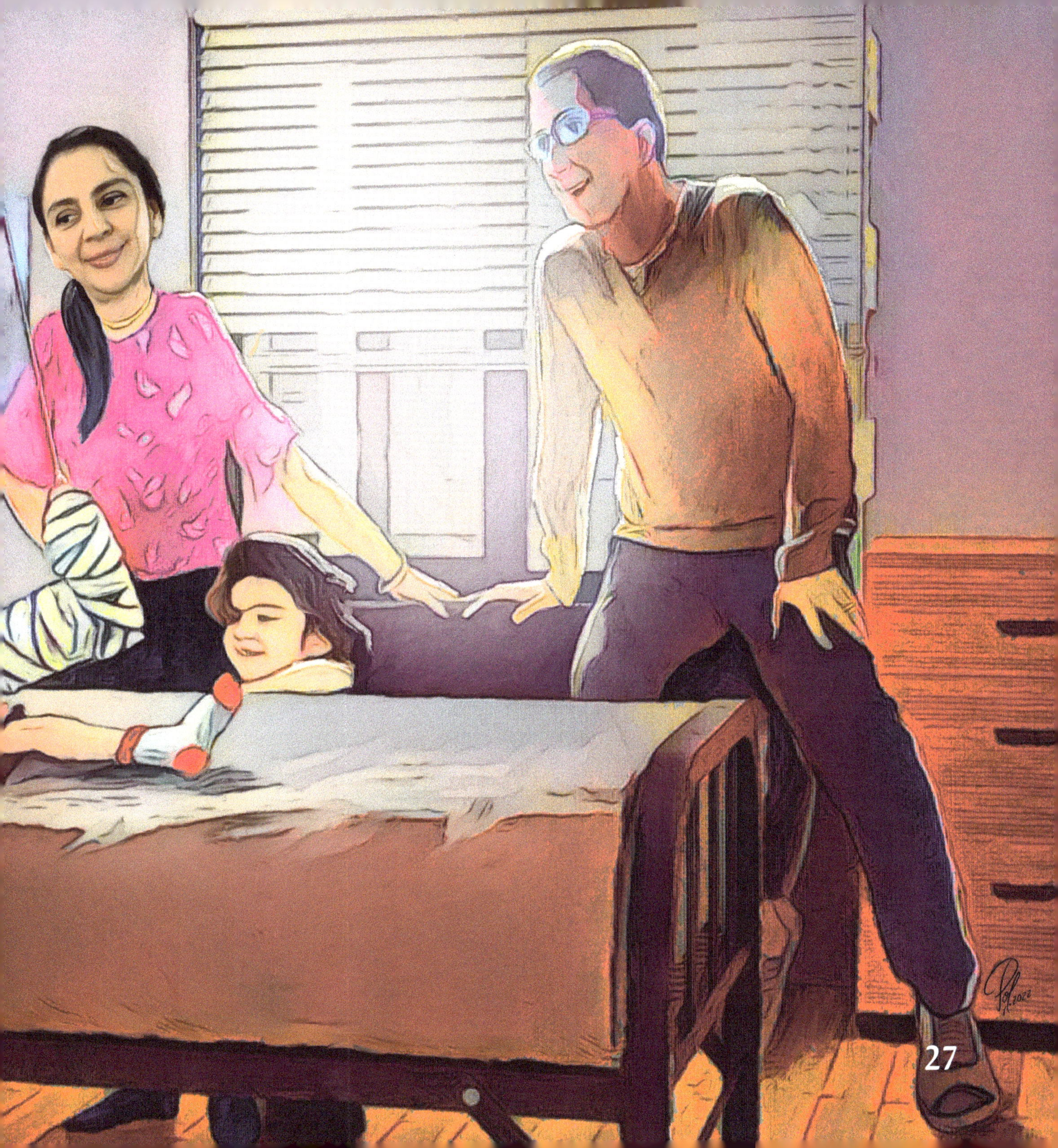

"No is what kept you from getting sick
eating way too many cookies."

"No is what kept you and your sister from what could have been a terrible accident."

"No is what kept you from daydreaming in class, so that you could learn to read, which will take you on many new adventures."

I sat down to think. Maybe
no *can* be a good word.

Sometimes, maybe no is
better than yes.

32

When my dog started to chase the neighbor's truck to the stop sign, I said, "Get out of the street, Simba...

33

34

ISBN 979-8-9886836-0-5

Text copyright © 2024 Brenda Novak, Inc.
Illustrations copyright © 2024 Pablo Ortega López
(polanimation.com)
Book design © 2024 Pablo Ortega López
(polanimation.com)

For information, address Brenda Novak, Inc., P.O. Box 3781,
Citrus Heights, CA 95611, USA.
www.brendanovak.com

9 789898 683605